STUDENT WORKBOOK

Office Procedures for the 21st Century

SEVENTH EDITION

Sharon Burton and Nelda Shelton

PEARSON

Prentice Hall

Upper Saddle River, New Jersey 07458

Pearson Prentice Hall™ is a trademark of Pearson Education, Inc.
Pearson® is a registered trademark of Pearson plc
Prentice Hall® is a registered trademark of Pearson Education, Inc.

Pearson Education LTD.
Pearson Education Singapore, Pte. Ltd.
Pearson Education Canada, Ltd.
Pearson Education–Japan
Pearson Education Australia PTY, Limited
Pearson Education North Asia Ltd.
Pearson Educación de Mexico, S.A. de C.V.
Pearson Education Malaysia, Pte. Ltd.

10 9 8 7 6 5 4 3 2 1
ISBN 0-13-232235-8

CONTENTS

PREFACE

Welcome to Supreme Appliances, Inc. As you will learn in Chapter 1, you will complete a part-time internship as an administrative assistant to support Amanda Quevedo, vice president of the Marketing Division at Supreme Appliances. After you complete your internship, you will be offered full-time employment as an administrative assistant to continue working with Ms. Quevedo in the Marketing Division.

The assignments you will receive will help you build skills that are required in today's office. The experience you will gain by performing a variety of tasks will help you to be prepared for the atmosphere and environment of a real office.

This packet contains the working papers you will need to complete the applications, which are included at the end of each chapter in the textbook. These working papers include forms, such as self-assessments, a job application form, telephone messages, and travel expense reports.

In addition to this packet of working papers, you will need the following items:

- Diskette to save your files
- File folders
- Three-ring binder
- Pens and pencils
- Paper for printing specific assignments

You will also need access to the following:

- A computer with Internet access
- A dictionary
- A copier/fax machine

Your success in completing the applications will depend on your readiness to:
- develop positive attitudes and visualize your need to prepare for successful employment.
- practice effective listening habits.
- develop working relationships with class members and your instructor.
- develop your thinking skills.
- deal with issues and problems of ethics and standards of personal conduct.
- develop a framework for building a successful and satisfying career.

IMPROVING YOUR WRITING SKILLS: PUNCTUATION WORKSHOP

Commas are used to set off words, phrases, and clauses in sentences. Complete the exercises below by applying punctuation rules for commas. Rules for all workshops are located in the Appendix.

For Review

Appendix: Rule 1: Commas Used with Conjunctions

Rule 2: Commas Used with Nonrestrictive Words, Phrases, and Clauses

Directions

Insert commas, if required, in the sentences below. Put a **C** at the end of the sentence if it is punctuated correctly.

Rule 1: Commas Used with Conjunctions

1. We carefully entered the data in the computers but the accounting clerk decided to double check our work.

2. A person should always take the time necessary to do every job well yet should be aware of the need to be efficient.

3. New application software usually comes stored on a CD-ROM disk but you can also request it on floppy disks as well.

4. Absenteeism is a problem in many offices and management constantly strives to reduce it.

5. "Just Say No" to drugs is a worthwhile program against drug abuse yet each year drug use continues to devastate our youth.

6. Applying for a job requires completing an application and submitting a resume each time you apply.

7. Digital cameras are becoming more popular and photo printers especially designed to print photos are now available on the market.

8. Printing envelopes is the last item on our list to do and we will be finished.

9. Flash drives are an excellent way to back up your documents in case your computer crashes and to have access to the files at work.

10. Output devices are used to get information from a computer and two of the most common output devices are a monitor and a printer.

Rule 2: Commas Used with Nonrestrictive Words, Phrases, and Clauses

1. To make traveling cheaper, families will often seek lodgings that do not include extras such as a pool or attached restaurant.

2. The manager who was recommended by the committee did not get the promotion.

3. The president is the one responsible of course for the final decision.

4. A delay in the morning mail whatever the reason may cause a delay at the bid-opening meeting.

5. John Curtis our production manager has been in that position for five years.

6. An application software program is a set of instructions written for a specific task such as word processing.

7. Your role as an office assistant when proofreading is to find errors and of course correct them.

8. Computer crime is becoming more and more a security issue and therefore cannot be ignored.

9. Ideally each employee should have an office that is ergonomically designed.

10. Unscheduled absenteeism is at an all time high because for example many employees feel that it is wasteful to not use all their sick leave.

OFFICE SUPPORT FUNCTIONS SELF-ASSESSMENT

Directions: Complete the self-assessment by placing a check mark in the box provided by those areas in which you feel you need improvement. Below the assessment, provide one suggestion on how you might improve each item.

Filing	☐	Handling messages/correspondence	☐
Photocopying	☐	Maintaining computer files/databases	☐
Keeping logs	☐	Critical thinking/decision-making skills	☐
Preparing documents	☐	Creating/analyzing reports	☐
Coordinating direct mailings	☐	Planning meetings and special events	☐
Using software applications	☐	Working closely with vendors/suppliers	☐
Giving presentations	☐	Making decisions concerning purchases	☐
Maintaining schedules	☐	People skills/working with others	☐
Maintaining calendars	☐	Coordinating a team project	☐
Interviewing techniques	☐	Planning, organizing, measuring	☐
Orienting and supervising	☐	Using the Internet for research	☐
Motivating staff	☐	Budgeting/staffing	☐
Evaluating personnel	☐	Problem solving	☐

List one suggestion about how you might improve each item you checked in this list. Identify the item followed by your suggestion.

NAME
DATE

IMPROVING YOUR WRITING SKILLS: PUNCTUATION WORKSHOP

Commas are used to set off words and phrases in sentences. Complete the exercises below by applying punctuation rules for commas.

For Review

Appendix: Rule 3: Commas Used with a Series
Rule 4: Commas Used between Adjectives
Rule 5: Commas Used with Introductory and Parenthetic Phrases

Directions

Insert commas, if required, in the sentences below. Circle the sentence number or key a **C**

at the end of the sentence if the sentence is punctuated correctly.

Rule 3: Commas Used with a Series

1. Please tell us when you plan to arrive at which hotel you will be staying and if you

   will need transportation to and from the meeting.

2. The faxes were from A. C. Produce Morgan Grocery and Henson Fish and Poultry

   Supply.

3. He went to the meeting and made the presentation.

4. We received three packages from three companies: AirExpress Overnight Transport

   and Fast 'n Fair.

5. The copier was giving us trouble and was repaired quickly.

6. Three personal qualities an office professional should possess are responsibility high

   self-esteem and integrity.

7. Gregg had experience in writing instruction manuals and in network management.

8. Shortly after the conference was over the assistants, Luisa Sanchez Alessandra

   Romano and Arnaud Beaufort passed out the session's evaluation forms.

9. You should recognize when more information is needed and decide where and how to look for it.

10. Our company has had little success trying to influence geographic population shifts in the economic environment or major cultural values.

Rule 4: Commas Used between Adjectives

1. The computer room must be a relatively cool dust-free room.

2. Ellen was an efficient effective employee.

3. Human resource managers want you to maintain a relaxed confident manner during an interview.

4. The filing system is an old outdated system.

5. The papers were handed out at the well-attended well-received conference.

6. Informal surveys may be conducted using small convenient samples.

7. The helpful very courteous usher took us right to our seats.

8. The uniform fit the driver well even though he had huge bulging muscles.

9. With one careful swift blow the jeweler cut the diamond exactly as he intended.

10. One manager visited a rival's store and spotted a colorful dramatic lighting display.

Rule 5: Commas Used with Introductory and Parenthetic Phrases

1. When an employee reaches age 55 he or she is eligible for retirement benefits.

2. The date of the meeting is March 15 rather than April 15.

3. Unless we receive written permission from the company the text may not be used.

4. He received an answer by fax after he sent the information.

5. We attended the conference of course because we had purchased our tickets.

6. For example retailers can evaluate new locations by observing vehicle and pedestrian traffic.

7. Today however many research studies appear to be little used because of the lack of time to adequately study the material.

8. Although a person's buying power is influenced by the amount of income he or she earns many consumers continue to purchase beyond their means.

9. Often purchasing a stripped-down model one without any extras is the best way to save the most money.

10. Early warning when a tornado has been sighted can save many lives.

DIVERSITY SELF-ASSESSMENT

Are you knowledgeable and understanding of diversity in your workplace? The following assessment will help you determine your strengths, as well as areas where you need improvement, as we begin our Diversity in the Workplace Workshop.

Directions

Place a check mark in the blank that best describes how you agree or disagree. Save the file.

	Agree	Somewhat Agree	Do Not Agree
1. I believe I understand cultural diversity.	_____	_____	_____
2. I communicate effectively with friends and coworkers from different backgrounds.	_____	_____	_____
3. I work well, or think I would work well, in diverse teams.	_____	_____	_____
4. I am familiar with other cultures' backgrounds and traditions.	_____	_____	_____
5. I avoid stereotyping other people.	_____	_____	_____
6. I can list all the areas of diversity in the workplace.	_____	_____	_____
7. I understand the role of gender in the workplace.	_____	_____	_____
8. I avoid all references in my language that could be interpreted as offensive to others.	_____	_____	_____

INTERPERSONAL SKILLS SELF-ASSESSMENT

Directions

Enter an **S** (strong), an **A** (average), or an **I** (needs improvement) in the Assessment column.

Skill		Assessment
1.	I easily recognize individual differences.	_____
2.	I can work with difficult people.	_____
3.	I enjoy teaching others.	_____
4.	I work as a team member.	_____
5.	I am willing to accept change.	_____
6.	I can exercise leadership.	_____
7.	I have good negotiation skills.	_____
8.	I embrace constructive criticism.	_____
9.	I keep confidential information confidential.	_____
10.	I demonstrate exceptional customer service.	_____

MEASURING YOUR SOFT SKILLS IQ

Directions: Place a check mark under the heading that represents the soft skill level you display on the job or would display on the job. The skills are in no particular order. Directions to score your Soft Skills IQ follow the assessment.

	Nonexistent	Poor	Average	Good	Excellent
Example: Commitment	___	___	√	___	___
1. Exhibit dependability.	___	___	___	___	___
2. Be self-motivated.	___	___	___	___	___
3. Exhibit positive self-esteem.	___	___	___	___	___
4. Exhibit self-management.	___	___	___	___	___
5. Display integrity and honesty.	___	___	___	___	___
6. Manage emotions under stress.	___	___	___	___	___
7. Demonstrate flexibility/adaptability.	___	___	___	___	___
8. Exhibit loyalty/commitment.	___	___	___	___	___
9. Exhibit pride.	___	___	___	___	___
10. Show creativeness.	___	___	___	___	___
11. Maintain clean/orderly/safe work area.	___	___	___	___	___
12. Demonstrate punctuality.	___	___	___	___	___
13. Recognize the need to change.	___	___	___	___	___
14. Display responsibility.	___	___	___	___	___
15. Follow rules and regulations.	___	___	___	___	___
16. Show willingness to learn.	___	___	___	___	___
17. Seek work challenges.	___	___	___	___	___
18. Demonstrate oral speaking ability.	___	___	___	___	___
19. Manage temperament.	___	___	___	___	___
20. Exhibit positive attitude and behavior.	___	___	___	___	___
21. Show empathy toward others.	___	___	___	___	___
22. Exhibit patience.	___	___	___	___	___
23. Pay attention to details to be accurate.	___	___	___	___	___
24. Practice good personal hygiene.	___	___	___	___	___
25. Project professional dress.	___	___	___	___	___

Scoring Scale:

1. To calculate your Soft Skills IQ, use the following scale:

   > 0 = Nonexistent
   > 1 = Poor
   > 2 = Average
   > 3 = Good
   > 4 = Excellent

2. Your total is your Soft Skills IQ.

3. Use the following scale to measure your IQ:

   > 90–100 = Excellent
   > 80–89 = Good
   > 70–79 = Average
   > 60–69 = Poor
   > 0–59 = You need to set specific goals and work to improve your IQ.

> **Is your Soft Skills IQ high enough to grab the attention of entry-level employers?**

RISK-TAKING ASSESSMENT
Recognizing Individual Differences

Directions: The purpose of this assessment is to help you identify your comfort with risk taking. Some of the examples are death-defying, others are only slightly risky. Let's see how close or far you are from death-defying. Place a check mark in the blank beside each statement you would consider doing.

		I Would Consider
1.	I would cross a railroad crossing when the crossing arms are down and the red lights are flashing, and I am in a hurry.	_____
2.	I would love to go bungee jumping.	_____
3.	I usually exceed the speed limit when driving long distances in my car.	_____
4.	I don't always buckle my seatbelt while driving.	_____
5.	I would love to go cave diving or have done so.	_____
6.	I would like to parachute out of an airplane.	_____
7.	It would be fun to walk across a long rope bridge that swings across a deep cavern.	_____
8.	I would ride a motorcycle without a helmet.	_____
9.	I would attempt to cross a roadway covered in over two feet of fast-moving water to save having to take the long way around to go home.	_____
10.	I would not worry about driving my car without car insurance.	_____

Scoring. Each item is worth 10 points. Count your check marks and multiply by 10 to arrive at your risk-taking percent.

Are you much of a risk taker?

Source: Adapted from "The Risk-Taking Scale" from *Human Relations: Interpersonal Job-Oriented Skills,* Andrew J. DuBrin, Pearson Prentice Hall, 2007.

NAME
DATE

FORM 2-D

IMPROVING YOUR WRITING SKILLS: CAPITALIZATION WORKSHOP

Letters are capitalized for two basic reasons: (1) to show the beginning of a sentence and (2) to show that a proper noun or adjective is more important than a common noun.

Complete the exercises below by applying the capitalization rules.

For Your Review

Appendix: Rule 6: Business Titles

Rule 7: Organizations, Institutions, and Education

Directions

Write *C* at the end of the sentence if the capitalization is correct. If the sentence is incorrect, use a proofreader's mark to make the necessary corrections.

Rule 6: Business Titles

1. The advisory committee to president Martin quickly approved the sale of the property.

2. Our main reason for setting the appointment at 8 a.m. was so Gregg Evers, our comptroller, could attend.

3. Danielle Sterns, president of Sterns & Sterns, is a very respected attorney.

4. Our Mayor, Ruth Steinback, spoke at the Executive Assistants Annual Conference.

5. Please send a copy of the proposal to Jonathan Hatfield, president, Hatfield and Associates.

6. Before your next meeting, contact your supervisor.

7. Please consult with the Director of Marketing, Iggis Mogarity, before sending the report.

8. Neither the chairperson nor the CEO were asked about the new mission statement.

9. The executive assistant was asked to serve on the new employee orientation committee.

10. Board chairman Klinkersmith follows the president on the agenda.

Rule 7: Organizations, Institutions, and Education

1. San Francisco hopes to host the republican national convention in the future.

2. Our American Records Management Association meeting was held last month at the Dunston hotel.

3. The senior class officers presented a skit in english.

4. Mr. Gordon, our managing editor, encouraged all employees to seek their bachelor or master's degree.

5. The local police department provided security at the Democratic national convention.

6. The national association of virtual assistants will be well represented at the next technology convention.

7. Dalworth College offers six programs in its computer information technology department.

8. The chamber of commerce has scheduled its next membership drive in March.

9. The Prescott Parent-Teacher Association meets monthly on Tuesday evening beginning at 7 p.m.

10. Students must enroll in the marketing course.

SELF-APPRAISAL INVENTORY
Answer the following questions in preparation for developing your resume.

PART I: PERSONAL INFORMATION	
Name	
Address	
Telephone	
Fax	
E-mail	

PART II: EMPLOYMENT BACKGROUND

Use action verbs to write sentences that list your work-related accomplishments.
Begin your sentences with some of the following verbs.

Earned	Developed	Supervised	Organized
Designed	Improved	Analyzed	Trained
Established	Managed	Prepared	Researched

1.
2.
3.
4.
5.
6.

Think of all the employment you have had, both career-related and other.
Use reverse chronological order (most recent first) to record your answers.

Working Title	
Company Name	
City Where Company Is Located	
Date Commenced and Ended	
Key Responsibilities	
Working Title	
Company Name	
City Where Company Is Located	
Date Commenced and Ended	
Key Responsibilities	

Continue to record information about your employment.	
Working Title	
Company Name	
City Where Company Is Located	
Date Commenced and Ended	
Key Responsibilities	

PART III: EDUCATION AND TRAINING

Use reverse chronological order to record the following information.
Use this area to record post-secondary education (full-time, extension, adult education, etc.)

Degree/Diploma/Certificate Earned	
Name of Institute	
City Where School Is Located	
Date Commenced and Ended	
Grade Point Average	
Key Courses Completed	

Use this area to record information about your high school education.

Diploma/Certificate Earned	
Name of School	
City Where School Is Located	
Date Commenced and Ended	
Grade Point Average	

PART IV: INTERESTS AND ACTIVITIES

List professional organizations that you have held or currently hold membership.	1. 2. 3.
List volunteer positions you have held or currently hold in your community.	1. 2. 3.
List sports or hobbies in which you participate	1. 2. 3.

NAME
DATE

APPLICATION FOR EMPLOYMENT

PERSONAL INFORMATION

Social Security No. _____

	Last	First	Middle
NAME:			

	Street	City	Province	Postal Code
ADDRESS:				

PHONE: _____ FAX: _____ E-MAIL: _____

REFERRED BY: _____

If related to anyone in our employ, state name and department: _____

TYPE OF EMPLOYMENT DESIRED

POSITION: _____ When can you start? _____ Salary Desired _____

Are you employed now? _____ May we contact your present employer? _____

EDUCATION	Name and Location of School	Years Attended	Date Graduated	Major Subjects
UNIVERSITY				
COLLEGE				
HIGH SCHOOL				
OTHER				

List specialized courses _____

_____

What foreign languages do you speak fluently? _____ Read? _____ Write? _____

NAME
DATE

FORM 3-B

FORMER EMPLOYMENT (List employers, starting with last one first.)

Date Month and Year	Company Name and City	Salary	Position	Reason for Leaving
From				
To				
From				
To				
From				
To				

VOLUNTEER ACTIVITIES (List any community service or volunteer work you have done.)

	Position	Name of Organization	Date Commenced and Ended
1			
2			

MEMBERSHIP (List any professional organization you hold membership in.)

	Name of Organization	Position Held
1		
2		

REFERENCES (Give the names of three persons not related to you.)

	Name and Title	Address	Telephone	E-Mail	Years Acquainted
1					
2					
3					

I understand that misrepresentation or omission of facts called for in this application is cause for dismissal.

Date _____   Signature _____

CHECKLIST FOR YOUR JOB CAMPAIGN

Activity	Date Due	Date Submitted
1. Prepare a self-appraisal inventory (Form 3-A).		
2. Use a financial manual or directory, available in either the school or public library, or on the Internet, to prepare a concise report on a local company.		
3. From the placement office, obtain literature that may be helpful to you in your job campaign.		
4. Join a committee to study employment opportunities for administrative assistants in your community. Obtain literature and share your findings with committee members.		
5. Prepare a list of qualifications you plan to emphasize during job interviews. Prepare a list of questions you expect to be asked and their answers. Prepare a list of questions you want to ask the interviewer.		
6. Prepare a resume.		
7. As directed, write either a prospecting job application letter or a solicited job application letter.		
8. Edit your resume after your instructor has reviewed it.		
9. Prepare a portfolio displaying samples of your work.		
10. Study job advertisements. Analyze the advertisements for administrative assistants.		
11. Write an evaluation of your performance during an early job interview.		
12. Complete the job application form (Form 3-B).		
13. Prepare a job acceptance letter and a job refusal letter.		

NAME

DATE

IMPROVING YOUR WRITING SKILLS: CAPITALIZATION WORKSHOP

Letters are capitalized for two basic reasons: (1) to show the beginning of a sentence and (2) to show that a proper noun or adjective is more important than a common noun. Complete the exercises below by applying capitalization rules.

For Your Review

Appendix: Rule 8: Enumerations

Rule 9: Nouns and Adjectives

Directions

Write *C* at the end of the sentence if the capitalization is correct. Otherwise, make the necessary corrections.

Rule 8: Enumerations

1. The Board of Trustees decided on three issues: (1) the board will grant an across-the-board increase in salary for all employees. (2) all insurance premiums will be paid by the company as of January 1. (3) after five years of employment, each employee will receive four weeks of paid vacation.

2. Some important issues facing your company are

   1. layoffs

   2. high cost of insurance premiums

   3. Worker morale

3. The publication listed the two most important concerns employers are faced with as (1) absenteeism and (2) accidents on the job.

4. Each employee in our department is required to know

   1. word

   2. lotus 1–2–3

   3. basic writing rules

   4. keyboarding: 50 wpm

5. He asked (1) would she be available to begin work immediately, (2) would she accept the salary offered, and (3) would she supervise the office if asked.

6. Here are three physiological symptoms of stress:

   a.   headaches

   b.   high blood pressure

   c.   heart disease

7. The following behavioral symptoms are seen in people who have experienced stress: (1) Decreased productivity; (2) Increased absenteeism; and (3) Increased turnover.

8. What do these messages mean to you?

   a. Promptness

   b.   being early

   c. Being the first one there

9. Your group is to answer three questions: What does it mean? do you agree? what are examples of this situation?

10. Discuss among yourselves:

    a. Are there any messages about the topic that come to mind?

    b. How many of these messages affect the group dynamics?

    c. How do you feel about these messages?

Rule 9: Nouns and Adjectives

1. The last act of the legislature was to pass public law 590, which increased the taxes on consumer goods.

2. Security nearest our office is precinct 12 of the Dallas police department.

3. The employees' credit union put on a comedy play called "Fast Money" in which the audience was given $1 each in act III.

4. The regulation in section F identified the steps we were to follow to investigate the problem.

5. She was grade 12, and he was grade 9.

6. The great depression is still studied because lessons can still be learned.

7. In many instances, the First Lady creates trends and establishes standards for women.

8. You may refer to the Net or the Internet.

9. We will meet next month in Building A, room 412, which is a larger room.

10. Not everyone knows how to write roman numerals beyond 20.

Using the notes in Application 4-A, print the work to be done and assign priorities to the items.

DAILY PLAN CHART

Date: _____

Rank	Calls to	Phone No.	Notes	Rank	Reminders

Rank	Letters and Memos to	Notes	Rank	Other Tasks

Priority Rank: 1, urgent; 2, today; 3, as soon as time allows

NAME
DATE

FORM 4-A

EVALUATION FORM

Directions

Use the following evaluation to rate your work and time management by marking *A* (always), *S* (sometimes), *N* (never) following each question.

1.   Do I complete tasks as efficiently as possible?

2.   Do I divide large projects into manageable segments of work?

3.   Do I group related tasks to reduce the time consumed in changing from one unrelated task to another?

4.   Do I match the work to the time frames in which it must be performed?

5.   Do I get organized before I begin an assignment?

6.   Do I control my attitudes and emotions that have a tendency to steal time?

7.   Do I prioritize my work into categories?

8.   Do I know how much time it takes to complete a task?

9.   Do I know if the task to be completed is a priority of my immediate supervisor?

10.   Do I maintain a TO DO list?

Give yourself the following points for your responses:

    2 points = ALWAYS
    1 point = SOMETIMES
    0 point = NEVER

If you have 20 points, you are a star manager of your work and time! If you have 16 points or higher, you are above average in managing your work and time. If you have 12–15 points, you need improvement in your management skills. If you have 11 points or fewer, you will not be recognized as being either effective or efficient.

NAME   FORM 4-B
DATE

STRESS ASSESSMENT

Stress is a necessary part of living. When you get up in the morning, you may not have enough time to do all the things you want to do. As you travel to work, you may experience additional stress. As you cope with a wide range of demands in your work environment, you experience additional stress. At times it seems that virtually everything causes stress!

Stress is not entirely bad; it can provide stimulation. Think about those stressful events that can be relaxing and exhilarating, such as taking a vacation or getting a new job. However, prolonged emotional and "wear-and-tear" experiences can lead to distress or anxiety. People must have opportunities to restore the emotional and physical resources that it takes to cope with stressful situations.

An accumulation of a variety of stresses can lead to nervousness, irritability, and fatigue, which in turn can affect your work, home, and personal life. The accumulation of stress on the job decreases worker motivation, quality of relationships, concentration and attention span, participation, general attitude, and enthusiasm. How intense is the stress in your life?

In Parts A and B, rate the following items from 1 (representing no stress) to 5 (representing extreme discomfort from stress).

Part A: Primary Concerns

1. Financial problems
2. Lack of time
3. Deadlines
4. Your health
5. Imbalance in major areas of your personal life (career, spiritual, family)

   6. Fear of failing
   7. Dull, boring life
   8. Social obligations
   9. Coping with family relationships
 10. Other

Part B: Symptoms

1. Need for more sleep
2. Headache
3. Feeling of exhaustion
4. Forgetfulness
5. Impatience

   6. Mood swings
   7. Always rushed
   8. Shaky feeling
   9. Digestive distress
 10. Other

Part C: Summary

1. List the three concerns that cause you the most discomfort.

   a. _____

   b. _____

   c. _____

2. List the three symptoms that cause you the highest discomfort.

    a. _____

    b. _____

    c. _____

3. List three things you intend to do to relieve the stress.

    a. _____

    b. _____

    c. _____

IMPROVING YOUR WRITING SKILLS: CAPITALIZATION WORKSHOP

Letters are capitalized for two basic reasons: (1) to show the beginning of a sentenc and (2) to show that a proper noun or adjective is more important than a common noun. Complete the exercises below by applying capitalization rules.

For Your Review

Appendix: Rule 10: Money

Rule 11: Geographical Terms

Rule 12: Government and Political Terms

Directions

Write *C* at the end of the sentence if the capitalization is correct; otherwise, make the necessary corrections.

Rule 10: Money

1. A check in the amount of one thousand forty-two dollars ($1,042.00) was mailed to you today.

2. The company profits were over $50,000.

3. The estate ran the company and paid dividends of five hundred sixty dollars ($560.00) to each stockholder.

4. When the auditor finished the report, he found that over $600.00 was missing.

5. The fee for use of said property is to be three hundred fifty dollars ($350.00) a month and is to be paid by June 15. (Legal document)

6. They wrote the check for incorrectly for two hundred dollars ($200).

7. The last line in the document should read two hundred fifty dollars ($250).

8. Their losses were over five thousand dollars' worth of merchandise.

9. The deal was worth only a few million dollars.

10. The player signed for 10.2 million dollars.

Rule 11: Geographical Terms

1. Our headquarters is on the west coast.

2. The south central part of the United States is sometime called the bible belt.

3. The Higgins building is located six blocks North on Fifth and Elm Streets.

4. Our company moved to Western Colorado because of the economic growth in that area.

5. The regional office located on the Florida coast is planning an expansion.

6. Betty Jo from the San Francisco office will be moving to the East Coast next summer.

7. If you want to go two blocks West, you must turn to the left at the next corner.

8. The new office building is located at the corner of North Hampshire and Collins Boulevard, just east of the river.

9. The local newspaper reports great growth in the south because of the nanotechnology industry.

10. Last winter the product development team moved its entire operations to the north of the city.

Rule 12: Government and Political Terms

1. Our federal reserve system is the central banking system of the United States.

2. Our national parks provide tremendous entertainment to millions of people.

3. The Water District has approved new regulations for the next fiscal year.

4. Statewide reforms are being carried out throughout Washington State.

5. The board of health has been reviewing the fruit and vegetable quarantines.

6. Their school district did not allow their employees to pay into social security until five years ago.

7. The War on Poverty has yet to be won.

8. Our retired employees are receiving their social security checks.

9. Although the Medicare Act has been very helpful, many people are still confused by its benefits.

10. Recently the New Boston city council held five closed-door meetings.

TELEPHONE MESSAGE FORMS

Urgent ❏
_____

Message For:

For _____

Date _____ Time _____

Message From:

M _____

Of _____

Phone _____

     AREA CODE   NUMBER   EXTENSION

Called while you were out ❏	Please call ❏
Stopped to see you ❏	Will call you back ❏
Returned your call ❏	Wishes to see you ❏

Message _____
_____
_____
_____
_____
_____
_____

Signed _____

FORM 5-A-1

Urgent ❏
_____

Message For:

For _____

Date _____ Time _____

Message From:

M _____

Of _____

Phone _____

     AREA CODE   NUMBER   EXTENSION

Called while you were out ❏	Please call ❏
Stopped to see you ❏	Will call you back ❏
Returned your call ❏	Wishes to see you ❏

Message _____
_____
_____
_____
_____
_____
_____

Signed _____

FORM 5-A-2

Urgent ❏
_____

Message For:

For _____

Date _____ Time _____

Message From:

M _____

Of _____

Phone _____

     AREA CODE   NUMBER   EXTENSION

Called while you were out ❏	Please call ❏
Stopped to see you ❏	Will call you back ❏
Returned your call ❏	Wishes to see you ❏

Message _____
_____
_____
_____
_____
_____
_____

Signed _____

FORM 5-A-3

Urgent ❏
_____

Message For:

For _____

Date _____ Time _____

Message From:

M _____

Of _____

Phone _____

     AREA CODE   NUMBER   EXTENSION

Called while you were out ❏	Please call ❏
Stopped to see you ❏	Will call you back ❏
Returned your call ❏	Wishes to see you ❏

Message _____
_____
_____
_____
_____
_____
_____

Signed _____

FORM 5-A-4

NOTES

FORM 5-B-1

NOTES

TELEPHONE SERVICES

Directions

Answer the following questions. Research for all answers should be gathered from either your local telephone directory or an online telephone directory.

1. List the following emergency numbers.
   a. Fire
   b. Police
   c. Your doctor
   d. Relative/Neighbor/Friend

2. List the following general information numbers.
   a. Gas trouble
   b. Power trouble
   c. Water trouble
   d. Time

3. List the area codes for the following locations.
   a. Your town or city
   b. Three major cities in your state

4. In what part of the telephone directory or online do you find local government listings?

5. If you want to inquire about obtaining or renewing a driver's license, what number would you call?

6. List the names and telephone numbers for two travel agencies in your town or city.

7. List the name, address, and telephone number for a professional moving and storage company located in your town or city.

8. If you place a call when your local time is 6 p.m. (1800), what time is it in the offices located in the following cities?
   a. Dallas
   b. San Francisco
   c. Chicago
   d. Calgary
   e. Miami
   f. Boston

9. If all the offices referred to in question 8 kept office hours of 9 a.m. to 5:30 p.m. (0900 to 1730), which offices would be open when you placed your call at 6 p.m. (1800) your local time?

10. List the names and telephone numbers for two local pharmacies in your town or city.

TELEPHONE DIALOGUES

Telephone Dialogue #1

EMPLOYEE:	Marketing Division. This is Lisa. May I help you?
CALLER:	Can you tell me the official title and mailing address of Richard Little?
EMPLOYEE:	Mr. Little doesn't work in this division, but if you don't mind holding for a moment, I can find that information for you.
CALLER:	Thank you.
EMPLOYEE:	Mr. Little's official title is Chief Financial Officer, Supreme Appliances, Inc. (pause). His mailing address is P.O. Box 7290, (pause) Rochester, NY (pause) 14623-7290. Did you get all that?
CALLER:	Yes. Thank you. You've have been very helpful.
EMPLOYEE:	I'll transfer you there.

Positive Comments   *Negative Comments*

NAME   **FORM 5-D**
DATE

Telephone Dialogue #2

EMPLOYEE:	Good afternoon. Marketing Division. This is Lisa. How may I help you?
CALLER:	I have just tried to call Kirk Lawrence and got someone else's extension.
EMPLOYEE:	Yes?
CALLER:	Do you have his direct telephone number?
EMPLOYEE:	Yes. That number is Extension 6402. Would you like me to transfer you to that extension?
CALLER:	Yes. Thank you.
EMPLOYEE:	I am transferring you there now. Thank you for calling.

Positive Comments   *Negative Comments*

Telephone Dialogue #3

EMPLOYEE:	Good morning. Marketing Division. This is Lisa. How may I help you?
CALLER:	May I speak with Amanda Quevedo, please?
EMPLOYEE:	Ms. Quevedo is not at her desk at the moment. May I take a message and ask her to return your call?
CALLER:	Yes. My name is David Solter.
EMPLOYEE:	How do you spell that?
CALLER:	S – O – L – T – E – R.
EMPLOYEE:	I'm sorry, is the first letter "F" or "S"?
CALLER:	"S" as in Sally.
EMPLOYEE:	Thank you. Is there a number where you can be reached?
CALLER:	In Washington, it's 202-555-2345.
EMPLOYEE:	That's David Solter at 202-5552345?
CALLER:	That's right.
EMPLOYEE:	Is there a message that you would like me to leave for Ms. Quevedo?
CALLER:	Please tell her that I called.
EMPLOYEE:	I'll make sure that Ms. Quevedo gets the message. Thank you for calling.

Positive Comments   *Negative Comments*

IMPROVING YOUR WRITING SKILLS: NUMBER USE WORKSHOP

To make a document look professional, numbers should be used in a consistent manner.

Do not spell out numbers in one section of a document and use figures in another section.

As a general rule, spell out numbers ten and under; use figures for numbers over ten.

For Review

Appendix: Rule 13: Numbers One through Ten

Rule 14: Dates

Rule 15: Percentages

Directions

Write *C* at the end of the sentence if the number use is correct. Otherwise, make the necessary corrections.

Rule 13: Numbers One through Ten

1. Tomorrow we will hire three accounting clerks, eleven packers, and seven drivers.

2. The new employee is on a six months' training program.

3. Nearly 300 people have been laid off from their jobs in the plant.

4. Over two hundred people will attend the conference next month.

5. Their new address is 7098-A 5th Avenue, Dallas, TX 75234.

6. On the CD-ROM, you should find at least twenty lessons.

7. Of the 125 pets rescued, approximately thirty will need medical attention.

8. In the nine-month training program, 17 trainees will complete their program early.

9. She made an error in her mailing street address; please correct the address to read as follows: 1408 3rd Avenue.

10. On March 10, the crew moved over 125 boxes to the new offices on the fourth floor.

Rule 14: Dates

1. The computer user groups will meet on April 10th.

2. The engineers will meet for their monthly meeting on the fifteenth.

3. The staff meeting will be on 7 September.

4. The invoice is due on the first of each month.

5. Please see that all e-mail notices are sent by March 15.

6. I closed my account the 2 of January.

7. Our sale will end on the 22nd of March.

8. The contract was mailed on the 5th of June.

9. Please let me hear from you by the 15th.

10. Do not expect our contract before the 15th of June.

Rule 15: Percentages

1. We want an increase of five percent in sales next month.

2. At least 25% of the participants agreed to the changes in the program for the next meeting.

3. We have received only 7.8% interest on our investment.

4. The new product requires at least 12 percent of the market share.

5. The computer prices have dropped by 10%.

6. Last year the department's budget increased at least 5.8 percent.

7. Our department expects at least 6.9 percent increase in productivity.

8. Our employees expect at least a 3.8% increase in pay for the coming year.

9. We mail 195 invitations and thus far have received at least nine percent responses.

10. We were told that at least 9% of the sales would be returned during the first week of the year.

RESERVATIONS FOR SEMINAR
Progress Report

Reservations have been con firmed at the Splendid Hotel for a meeting room and a

luncheon for Friday Nov. 16, from nine until five o'clock. for the seminar on

"Supervising Employee."

The meeting room, called the Rose Garden, will seat 125 people. The room is well

lighted, beautifully Decorated, and faces the rose garden. The chairs are comfortable.

While I was at the splendid hotel, I asked about parking space and I talked with the

banquet mgr. about a luncheon menu. Parking space isadequate. Mr. Lawrence, the

banquet mgr., gave me a choice of menus. The ist of choices are attached. Do you have a

perference? We must give a form com mitment on the number who will attend the

luncheom by 10 oclock the day of the luncheon.

LETTER COPY

1. Mr. Raymond Jones, Plant Manager, Southwestern Manufacturing Plant, Supreme Appliances, Inc, 2600 W. Vickery Boulevard, Fort Worth, TX 76102-7105. Dear Raymond: The demand for freezers is so great this season that we are offering the 20-cubic-foot freezer for only $50 more than the 16-cubic-foot freezer. (P)* As you are aware, our supply of 16-cubic-foot freezers is almost exhausted. Many more have been sold since our conversation yesterday. The demand for the 20-cubic-foot freezer will increase rapidly. (P) This letter is your authorization to ship thirty 20-cubic-foot freezers to each of our four regional sales offices immediately. Sincerely yours, Amanda Quevedo, Vice President, Marketing cc Mr. John Reddin (Mr. Reddin's address is Mr. John Reddin, Manager, Sales Office, Southwestern Region, 1508 Commerce Street, Dallas, TX 75201-4904.)

2. Mr. Kyle Rhodes, Manager, Western Region Sales Office, Supreme Appliances, Inc., 1400 Lincoln Street, Denver, CO 80203-1523. Dear Mr. Rhodes: At Thursday's meeting of the Executive Committee of the National Sales Association, we selected the speakers we hope will accept our invitation to participate in our annual sales conference from March 16 to March 20 in Chicago. (P) Several of the council members said they heard you speak last year at the Western Division of Administrative Managers and recommended you be invited to give the keynote address at the spring conference of the National Sales Association on Tuesday, March 16, at 10:30 a.m. in the Luxury Hotel, Chicago. Your expenses will be paid, and you will receive an honorarium. (P) Will you accept our invitation to be the keynote speaker? Sincerely, Amanda, Quevedo, Program Chairperson.

3. Mr. Michael Carter, 1515 Beech Avenue, Suite 10, Chicago, IL 60601-3214. Dear Mr. Carter: Plans for the March conference of the National Sales Association are complete, and we can look forward to a motivating and challenging conference. (P) Thank you for meeting and evaluating the ideas for the conference. You contributed many ideas that were incorporated into the program. (P) I am looking forward to the week of March 16-20 in Chicago. I will see you there. Send copies to: Henry Pippin, J. R. Rush, Thomas Strickland, Sid Levine, and Karen Baxter. (Refer to the Introduction to Supreme Appliances in Chapter 1, for addresses.)

*(P) means make a new paragraph.

SA Supreme Appliances, Inc.

14 Shady Lane, Rochester, NY 14623

NAME

DATE

SA Supreme Appliances, Inc.

14 Shady Lane, Rochester, NY 14623

SA Supreme Appliances, Inc.

14 Shady Lane, Rochester, NY 14623

NAME

DATE

FORM 6-C-4

IMPROVING YOUR WRITING SKILLS: NUMBER WORKSHOP

To make a document look professional, numbers should be used in a consistent manner.

Do not spell out numbers in one section of a document and use figures in another section.

As a general rule, spell out numbers ten and under; use figures for numbers over ten.

For Review

Appendix: Rule 16: Time

                     Rule 17: Serial and Similar Numbers

Directions

Write *C* at the end of the sentence if the number use is correct. Otherwise, make the necessary corrections.

Rule 16: Time

1. The meeting was scheduled for 3:00 p.m., and the refreshments arrived at 3:15 p.m.

2. I will present my topic at 4 p.m.

3. Our pre-meeting party will begin at 6 o'clock and dinner will be served at 7:00 p.m.

4. Their appointments were scheduled 15 minutes apart as shown here: 4:15 p.m.; 4:30 p.m.; 4:45 p.m.; 5:00 p.m.

5. The three executives will arrive at 7 o'clock.

6. The project took two years and three months.

7. The group of international visitors was to arrive by 7PM.

8. Because the team was delayed in traffic, the meeting will begin at six-thirty o'clock.

9. Employees are being notified to attend a meeting this morning at 10:00.

10. At 10:00 a.m. this morning, the trainer for the Spanish classes was to begin the class.

Rule 17: Serial and Similar Numbers

1. They measured the filing storage space to be eight feet by eight feet.

2. As a team, their weight loss was 125 pounds.

3. The blouses, style 4513, were found in the box marked as skirts.

4. The special delivery package weighed 2 pounds 11 ounces.

5. The calculator, serial no. 2–145–9087, was reported missing on June 14.

6. The printer is marked as Model II-XL-A and the Serial No. is 666–545–798.

7. They needed caps in serial no. 15–8977–12, not in 15–8077–12.

8. They paid Invoice no. 43219 in ten days and received the 2 percent discount.

9. To show their support, the office workgroup ordered a half-dozen blue oxford shirts, size 17/33.

10. The last number to be entered into the database was policy fourteen.

NOTES ON INCOMING MAIL FOR MONDAY, JULY 14

1. The August issue of *Sales and Marketing Management.*

2. A personal letter for Karen Baxter.

3. A complaint from a customer in the Southwestern Region. The copper-tone of the new dishwasher she had installed does not match her other copper-tone appliances.

4. A letter to A. Quevedo asking her to speak at the International Conference of the Society of Administrative Management.

5. An e-mail from Microwave Ovens, Inc. saying the catalog A. Quevedo has requested is out of print and will be mailed as soon as it is off the press.

6. The July issue of *Internet World.*

7. An e-mail from the Human Resources Department on new personnel policies for Supreme Appliances, Inc.

8. An e-mail from the sales office in Portland, Oregon, saying the demand for appliances in harvest gold is twice as great as that for appliances in other colors. What can be done to increase the shipments of harvest gold appliances?

9. The August issue of *Administrative Management.*

10. A letter from a customer in Denver complaining that the surface on the hood installed with her new electric range is peeling. Will Supreme Appliances replace the hood?

11. A sales letter from Microwave Ovens, Inc. on the new features of their latest microwave oven.

12. An e-mail from the manager of the Western Manufacturing Plant offering suggestions for speeding up delivery of appliances after they are manufactured.

13. An e-mail from the sales office in Boston saying that the demand for appliances in harvest gold is twice as great as that for appliances in other colors. Send more harvest gold appliances.

14. An e-mail from the Southwestern manufacturing plant saying that the parts ordered are not available and will have to be manufactured.

15. A letter from Maybelle Anderson giving the title of her talk for the November Sales Seminar.

16. A complaint from a customer in the Eastern Region. She is dissatisfied with her electric range, which is only two years old, because the element in the oven burned out. Will Supreme Appliances replace the element?

17. A request from Supreme Executive Vice President asking for a comparative sales report for the past five years.

18. An expiration notice for *Administrative Management*.

19. A letter from the local Chamber of Commerce asking A. Quevedo to serve as chairperson of the Community Development Committee.

20. An e-mail from Jack Winfield canceling the appointment he has with A. Quevedo on Friday, August 22.

DAILY MAIL REGISTER

Date	Description	To Whom Sent	Action to Be Taken	Follow-up

NAME
DATE

FORM 7-A-2

TO DO LIST   TO DO LIST

NAME   **FORM 7-A-3**
DATE

ROUTING FORMS

Date_____				Date_____			
Routing Sequence	Person	Date	Initial	Routing Sequence	Person	Date	Initial
	K. Baxter				K. Baxter		
	S. Levine				S. Levine		
	J. Ross				J. Ross		
	T. Strickland				T. Strickland		
	Return to A. Quevedo				Return to A. Quevedo		

Date_____				Date_____			
Routing Sequence	Person	Date	Initial	Routing Sequence	Person	Date	Initial
	K. Baxter				K. Baxter		
	S. Levine				S. Levine		
	J. Ross				J. Ross		
	T. Strickland				T. Strickland		
	Return to A. Quevedo				Return to A. Quevedo		

LIST OF OUTGOING MAIL

	Item	Class of Mail
1.	Typewritten checks	_____
2.	Handwritten letter	_____
3.	Keys	_____
4.	Package weighing three pounds	_____
5.	Business reply cards	_____
6.	Photocopy of a letter	_____
7.	Bills and statements	_____
8.	Merchandise to be delivered on Sunday	_____
9.	Photocopy of a letter	_____
10.	Regularly issued periodicals	_____
11.	Catalog with 26 bound pages	_____
12.	A film sent to a school	_____
13.	Typewritten letter	_____
14.	Magazines	_____
15.	Material sealed against postal inspection	_____

NAME
DATE

LIST OF EXTRA OUTGOING MAIL SERVICES

<u>Item</u>   <u>Extra Service</u>

Evidence of mail; must be
purchased at time
of mailing; items using this
service must be
1. presented at a post office.   _____

Provides date and time of
delivery or
attempted delivery and name of
person who
2. signed for item.   _____

Provides date and time of
delivery or
attempted delivery; must be
purchased at
3. time of mailing only.   _____

Provides coverage against loss of
damage
up to $5,000; items must not be
insured for
4. more than value.   _____

Provides proof of mailing at time
of
mailing and date and time of
delivery or
attempted delivery; a record is
maintained
5. by USPS.   _____

NAME   **FORM 7-C**
DATE

Provides for up to $500 coverage and is based on amount of coverage needed up to $500.

6. _____

Provides sender with a mailing receipt and a return receipt;

7. record is maintained by USPS. _____

Provides maximum protection and security for valuables; must be presented to a post office or a

8. rural carrier. _____

Permits a mailer to direct delivery only to addressee or addressee's authorized agent. Addressee must be an individual specified by

9. name. _____

Provides sender a postcard or electronic notification, via fax or e-mail with date of delivery and

10. recipient's signature. _____

MAIL OPERATIONS—Field Trip Activity

Location _____

Date _____

Contact Person _____

Title _____

Incoming Mail:

1. Where does the mail enter the building?
2. What happens to it then?
3. How is it distributed through your offices and how often?
4. Which personnel handle the mail?
5. From the time the mail arrives at your receiving door, how long does it take to distribute it?
6. How do you report errors made using the postage meter?
7. Do you log any information in a record book when you use the postage meter, or do you receive a printout.
8. What kind of information does the postage meter provide?

Outgoing Mail:

1. How is the outgoing mail consolidated?
2. How is it prepared—wrapped, labeled, stamped, etc.?
3. How is it divided into classes of mail?
4. How often is it taken to the post office?
5. Is it scheduled to meet outbound postal schedules?

General Procedures:

1. How do you obtain a postage meter?
2. What steps should everyone take to eliminate expensive mailing costs?
3. Since your organization is using e-mail and faxes, have you noticed a decrease in the amount of mail being distributed among departments or outgoing?
4. How much mail makes a postage meter practical?
5. How do you think your employees can improve their preparation of mailings?
6. What special equipment is needed to have in a small company to prepare the mailings?
7. What are the most important reference manuals you use in your mailroom?
8. Do you create any type of mailing usage report for your organization?
9. What trends will affect mail operations?

IMPROVING YOUR WRITING SKILLS: GRAMMAR WORKSHOP

Are you the person everyone comes to when they have a question about grammar rules? You should want to be that person. Those employees who are known as the "grammar gurus" are recognized as highly skilled. Excellent grammar skills can help your career advancement.

For Review

Appendix: Rule 18: Subject and Verb Agreement

Directions

Write *C* at the end of the sentence if the sentence is correct. Otherwise, make the necessary corrections.

Rule 18: Subject and Verb Agreement

1. Do the two children has separate insurance policies?

2. A set of specifications for the job are enclosed.

3. Several different opinions about the completion of the project were voiced at the staff meeting yesterday.

4. The president of the Dallas-based banks was at the meeting.

5. The ventures of Murray Investments Inc. was under investigation.

6. Amy Johnson has been employed as the director for several years.

7. You and I was to be commended for all our work on the project at the meeting on Friday.

8. Wal-Mart, Costco, and Target each has been recognized as the leaders in the retail market.

9. For over 40 years WRL has been helping people achieve their retirement dreams.

10. Dennis busted the piñata at our manager's birthday party.

INDEXING NAMES

Larsen James R (1) James R. Larsen	(2) Bob O'Donald
(3) Helen Vandermallie	(4) Martha Odell-Ryan
(5) Sister Edward	(6) Georgia Ann Harris
(7) Mrs. Georgia Harris	(8) Father Jenkins
(9) Ty Chen	(10) Martha Odellman
(11) Allen's Swap Shop	(12) J. T. Larson
(13) Herbert Vander Mallie	(14) George Haris
(15) Mary Allen's Beauty Shop	(16) Marshall Field & Company
(17) Georgia Harris	(18) Allens' Print Shop
(19) Trans-Continent Truckers	(20) George Harris
(21) James Larson	(22) Hubert Vander Mallie

(23) George E. Harris	(24) South Carolina Industries
(25) North East Fuel Supply	(26) AAA Batteries
(27) WHAM Radio	(28) Higgins Cleaners
(29) 24 Hour Grocery	(30) New Jersey Office Supply
(31) Over-30 Club	(32) Prince Arthur's Hair Styling
(33) Human Rights Division, Illinois	(34) First Baptist Church
(35) Hotel Isabella	

ALPHABETIZING NAMES
ANSWER SHEET

Alphabet	Number of Card	Alphabet	Number of Card
A		N	
B		O	
C		P	
D		Q	
E		R	
F		S	
G		T	
H		U	
I		V	
J		W	
K		X	
L	*1, 12*	Y	
M		Z	

NAME

DATE

INDEXING AND ALPHABETIZING NAMES

(36) James Danforth, Jr	(37) Burns Travel Agency
(38) Caddo County Water Department	(39) Norton R. Henson
(40) Sister Marie	(41) The Lone Ranger
(42) The Jefferson Party House	(43) El Rancho Inn
(44) Cecil Young-Jones	(45) RCT Manufacturers
(46) Administrative Management	(47) Hotel Baker
(48) Tri-State Enterprises	(49) Miss Robert's Charm School
(50) The Daily Oklahoman	(51) Bob Guerin

ALPHABETIZING NAMES
ANSWER SHEET

Alphabet	Number of Card	Alphabet	Number of Card
A		N	
B		O	
C		P	
D		Q	
E		R	
F		S	
G		T	
H		U	
I		V	
J		W	
K		X	
L		Y	
M		Z	

NAME

DATE

(52) William T. Au	(53) Thomas Kaplan, M. D.
(54) Irene McGregor	(55) Arthur P. Van der Linden
(56) College of Notre Dame	(57) John Wilkins Supply Corp.
(58) Southwestern Distributors	(59) Internal Revenue Service (Department of the Treasury)
(60) Four Corners Answering Service	(61) The University of Oklahoma
(62) Montgomery & Co.	(63) South East Pipeline
(64) Webbers' Home for the Aged	(65) People's Republic of China
(66) New Orleans Printing Co.	(67) Marine Midland Bank–Rochester
(68) Miss Laura's Candy Shop	(69) Strong Memorial Hospital
(70) Surv-Ur-Self Pastries, Inc.	

INDEXING AND ALPHABETIZING NAMES

(36) James Danforth, Jr	(37) Burns Travel Agency
(38) Caddo County Water Department	(39) Norton R. Henson
(40) Sister Marie	(41) The Lone Ranger
(42) The Jefferson Party House	(43) El Rancho Inn
(44) Cecil Young-Jones	(45) RCT Manufacturers
(46) Administrative Management	(47) Hotel Baker
(48) Tri-State Enterprises	(49) Miss Robert's Charm School
(50) The Daily Oklahoman	(51) Bob Guerin

NAME
DATE

(52) William T. Au	(53) Thomas Kaplan, M. D.
(54) Irene McGregor	(55) Arthur P. Van der Linden
(56) College of Notre Dame	(57) John Wilkins Supply Corp.
(58) Southwestern Distributors	(59) Internal Revenue Service (Department of the Treasury)
(60) Four Corners Answering Service	(61) The University of Oklahoma
(62) Montgomery & Co.	(63) South East Pipeline
(64) Webbers' Home for the Aged	(65) People's Republic of China
(66) New Orleans Printing Co.	(67) Marine Midland Bank–Rochester
(68) Miss Laura's Candy Shop	(69) Strong Memorial Hospital
(70) Surv-Ur-Self Pastries, Inc.	

ALPHABETIZING NAMES
ANSWER SHEET

Alphabet	Number of Card	Alphabet	Number of Card
A		N	
B		O	
C		P	
D		Q	
E		R	
F		S	
G		T	
H		U	
I		V	
J		W	
K		X	
L		Y	
M		Z	

NAME

DATE

INDEXING AND ALPHABETIZING
LIST OF NAMES

(71) Jason Wayne Suppliers	(72) General Insurance Company, Rochester, New York
(73) Prince Charles	(74) Federal Communications Commission
(75) Hank Christian	(76) East Avenue Baptist Church
(77) KRLD Radio	(78) Maudeen E. Livingston
(79) Jim Waldrop	(80) Social Security Administration (Department of Health and Human Services)
(81) The Royal Inn	(82) Human Rights Division of New York
(83) Ellen Jan Elgin	(84) Robert Edward Kramer, D.V.M.

(85) Robert E. Kramer	(86) United Hauling, Ltd.
(87) Prince James Portraiture	(88) Harold Roberson
(89) General Insurance Company Rochester, Minnesota	(90) First National Bank Chicago, Illinois, Oaks Branch
(91) Harold O. Roberson	(92) M C Tree Service (formerly Collier Tree Service)
(93) Mrs. Maudeen Livingston	(94) George Zimmer Corporation
(95) The Johns Hopkins University	(96) Rain or Shine Boot Shoppe
(97) M. T. Torres	(98) Marion Burnett
(99) Harold Robertson	(100) John R. de Work

(101) Del Monte Properties	(102) Mason-Dixon Consultants
(103) Robert Edwin Kramer, M.D.	(104) Ciudad Acuna Television Repair
(105) Pierre Chez	(106) North Carolina Pipeline
(107) Frank T. Forthright	(108) Bill Carter Petroleum Corporation
(109) General Insurance Company Amarillo, Texas	(110) First National Bank Chicago, Illinois, Aspin Branch

ALPHABETIZING NAMES
ANSWER SHEET

Alphabet	Number of Card	Alphabet	Number of Card
A		N	
B		O	
C		P	
D		Q	
E		R	
F		S	
G		T	
H		U	
I		V	
J		W	
K		X	
L	*1, 12*	Y	
M		Z	

CROSS-REFERENCING NAMES

Cross-Reference
See

Cross-Reference
See

Cross-Reference
See

Cross-Reference
See

DIRECTIONS FOR USING WINDOWS EXPLORER

The following directions will present how-to information on these operations in Windows Explorer:
- Expanding and collapsing drives and folders
- Displaying drive and folder contents
- Finding a file
- Copying a file
- Moving a file
- Deleting a file and restoring it from the Recycle Bin

As you learn about file management in the steps to follow, refer to the parts of Windows Explorer.

Based on your Windows version, the results may vary slightly from the steps given below.

 Access your Windows Explorer by:

1. Clicking on Start, and selecting All Programs, Accessories, Windows Explorer.
2. Sizing the window for your desired viewing. You can also size each of the vertical windows within the larger one to see all the information.

Parts of Windows Explorer
Think of the structure of this file management tool as a filing cabinet with folders inside of filing drawers. This concept is represented in Explorer with a "tree" type of appearance—directories come off main drives, files come off directories, etc.

On the left side of your Explorer window are the folders in your chosen drive. The Explorer view begins with Desktop, followed by My Computer, and lists all your drives, followed by other folders or programs contained within the Desktop and My Computer. Your directory structure is indicated by the indentation levels in Explorer's left pane. On the right side are the files and folders that are contained within the folder you select at left. Your selected folder appears to be open, with its contents spilling out into the right panel.

A minus symbol on a folder means that it is fully expanded. A plus symbol on a folder means that more files are contained inside it than are visible. When you click on the minus symbol, the folders collapse. To expand the folders, click on the plus symbol.

When you want to see details of your files (e.g., size, date created/modified), click on View, Details. When you just want to see a list of files, click on View, List. The parts of the Explorer window include the following:

- Drives
- Folders/Directories
- Subdirectories
- Files within Folders

 Practice moving around in the Explorer window by:

1. Clicking on the folders on the left side to see how the subfolders and files are displayed on the right side of the window.
2. Using the scroll bars in the windows to navigate.
3. Clicking on the items on the menu bar to see the options provided.
4. Identifying in your Explorer window all the parts identified previously.

Be sure you can expand and collapse folders and display folders/directories/files in different views.

Finding Files

If you save a file and then can't remember what you named it or where it was saved, you can search for the file using the Windows Search feature. Windows allows you to locate files based on file name, a portion of a name, date, and/or the text included in a file. To conduct a search, you can:

- Use your START menu and choose Search, Files and Folders (word processing, spreadsheets, etc.).
- Click on My Documents from the START menu, and click on Documents or All Files or Folders.
- Right-click on My Computer, and choose Search.
- Using a basic search, indicate the file name or a portion of the file name (if you don't know it all) and search either your entire computer or any drives or directories you choose.

Here are some examples of ways of searching:

- You saved a Word document to your hard drive [C:], but you can't remember the name or where it was saved (but would recognize it). The syntax for entering into the "Named:" box would be
  *.doc (will show all files with a .doc extension).
  *.ppt (will show all files with a .ppt extension).
- You want to find the file called "Project A-12," but you only remember part of the name – "Project." The syntax would be
  Project* (will show all files beginning with Project).

- In the Look in: box, click the Browse button and click on [C:] so that the search will start from the main level or root of the C: drive. To start the search, click on Search.

Your search results screen will list the file or files that match your criteria. The screen functions like a window in Explorer or My Computer. Here you may open, copy, move, and delete files.

 Practice using the Search tool:

1. Click on Start and click on Search.
2. In the Named: box, type *.doc
3. In the Look in: box, click Browse and select C:
4. Click on Search.

You should see all the documents with the .doc extension on your C: drive (hard drive). When you find a file you are searching for, you can double-click on the file name; it will launch the application and open your file.

Be certain you can locate your files using different methods.

Copying Files

You can use several methods for copying (and moving) files:

- Right-clicking
- Clicking a toolbar icon
- Clicking Edit, Copy on the menu bar
- Pressing "Ctrl C" on your keyboard
- Dragging your files to another location.

As you gain more experience and confidence, you will probably use the dragging option more frequently. Initially, you may prefer the other options.

Basically when copying files from one directory or drive to another, you select the file, then use one of these methods to copy it to another location.

 Try the following ways to copy files:

Right-clicking
1. Put a disk with <u>at least three expendable files to play with</u> in your A: drive.
2. Open Windows Explorer.

3. Click once on [A:] to reveal all the files on your disk (A: drive).
4. Right-click on one of the files and choose Copy.
5. On the left side, click on C: and navigate down to the Temp folder.
6. Right-click on Temp and choose Paste (left-click).
7. Check it by double-clicking on the Temp directory folder to see it displayed on the right side.

Menu Bar
1. Click once on a file on your disk (A:); on the menu bar, choose Edit, Copy.
2. Navigate to the directory folder where you wish to place your file (Temp). Select it by clicking on it once.
3. On the menu bar, choose Edit, Paste.
4. Check it by double-clicking on Temp to see it displayed on the right side.

Keyboard
1. Select a file on your A: drive (disk) by clicking on it once; press Ctrl c (hold down control while you press the letter c). Then release it—you have just copied it.
2. Navigate to the directory where you wish to place your file (Temp). Select it by left-clicking on Temp once.
3. Press Ctrl v (hold down control while you press v).
4. Check it by double clicking on Temp and see it displayed on the right.

Dragging

NOTE: You need both directories visible to use this option. Or you can open up Explorer again and move the windows around for good viewing.

1. In one window locate the file to be copied.
2. In the second window, scroll to the desired target drive and folder so it is visible.
3. Then click and hold the left mouse button on the file in the first window and drag it to the second window to the desired folder:
   a. If copying it to the same drive, hold down the letter c on your keyboard while you drag it. (Remember: C for copy!)
   b. If copying the file to a different drive, just drag it.
4. Drop it precisely on the folder to which it will go. A small box will be visible around the selected folder, so you can drop it within that folder. If you miss, check the folders above and below your selected folder to see where the file is located. Otherwise, you may have to search to locate it.

TIP: You can copy several files at a time by
   ■ Left-clicking on one file, holding down the Ctrl key while you select the other files
   ■ Releasing the Ctrl key and on any one of the selected files and dragging the file to the desired location.

Perform the Copy function using the following methods:

1. Click on A: to reveal your files on the right side.
2. Right-click on one of the files and choose Copy.
3. On the left, scroll down to the Temp folder, right-click on it. Choose Paste. See how easy it is!
4. Repeat the same steps, but this time select the file and click on Edit on the menu bar, then perform the copy and paste functions.

Now let's try copying several files from one drive to another using two windows:
1. Open Windows Explorer
2. Open Windows Explorer **again.**
3. On the task bar at the very bottom of the screen, find an open spot, right-click in that space and choose **Tile Windows Horizontally**. Now you have two windows open.
4. In the top window, click on A: to reveal your files on the right side.
5. In the bottom window, click on C: and scroll to the Temp folder.
6. In the top window, select three files by
7. Left-clicking on one file, hold down the Ctrl key while you select (left-click) two other files. Now you see three highlighted (selected) files.
8. Release the Ctrl key and on any one of the selected files, drag to the bottom window to the Temp folder. All three files were copied.

Moving Files
The process of moving files from one place to another is essentially the same as copying files. When right-clicking or choosing Edit from the menu,
■ Select your file.
■ Choose Cut instead of Copy.
■ Then go to the drive or directory where you want to move the file and select Paste.

*Note: Dragging files **only copies** files; they remain in two places. Also, remember you can move multiple files in the same manner as described under Copying Files.*

 Try moving a file by doing the following:

1. On the left, click on A: to reveal your files on the right side.
2. Right-click on one of the files and choose Cut.
3. Then scroll to your Temp directory on the left, right-click on Temp and choose Paste.
4. Now click once on that same file in Temp.
5. Click on Edit on the menu bar and choose Cut.
6. Now click on A: and on the menu bar, choose Edit, Paste.

Deleting Files

Deleting files and folders is easy—almost too easy. Here again, you have several options:

- Select the file or folder and click the *delete* icon on your toolbar.
- Select the file or folder and press the Delete key.
- Right-click the file or folder and choose Delete.
- Drag the file and drop it in the Recycle Bin (explained further in the next section) on your desktop.

Unless you have indicated in the Recycle Bin that you wish all files that you delete to be permanently deleted, and unless you are on a floppy drive, deleting will merely send your files to the Recycle Bin, from where you can permanently delete them later.

WARNING: When you delete a folder, you delete all files in that folder. Before deleting a folder, be sure that it does not contain files you wish to keep!

Try deleting files by doing the following: *be sure these files are your "play" files that can be trashed!*

1. Close one of the Explorer windows if still open.
2. Click on A: to reveal your files on the right side.
3. Left-click on one of the files to select it.
4. Press your Delete key on the keyboard.
5. Now select another file on A:
6. Copy that file to your Temp directory (according to previous instructions).
7. Double-click on the Temp folder to see the file.
8. Now left-click on that file to select it.
9. Drag the file to the Recycle Bin. *Remember, this file is not really gone yet. You can retrieve it. But once you empty the Bin, it is history!*

*Remember, **only files deleted from your hard drive can be retrieved from the Recycle Bin**.*

Be certain you are aware of your organization's records management procedures for deleting files. If you are in doubt about deleting certain files, be sure to ask your supervisor or let your supervisor know which files you are deleting that cannot be restored.

Restoring Files from the Recycle Bin

The Recycle Bin provides a safety net when deleting files or folders. When you delete any of these items from your hard disk, Windows places them in the Recycle Bin. The Recycle Bin icon changes from "empty" to "full." Items deleted from a floppy disk or a network drive are permanently deleted and are not sent to the Recycle Bin.

Items in the Recycle Bin remain there until you decide to permanently delete them from your computer. These items still take up hard disk space and can be undeleted or restored back to their original location.

To restore or delete files in the Recycle Bin, you can use one of the following options:
- To restore an item, right-click it and then click Restore.
- To restore all of the items, on the Edit menu, click Select All, and then on the File menu, click Restore.
- To delete an item, right-click it and then click Delete.
- To delete all the items, on the File menu, click Empty Recycle Bin.

 Try restoring the files in the Recycle Bin.

1. To restore an item, right-click it and then click Restore.
2. To restore all of the items, on the Edit menu, click Select All, and then on the File menu, click Restore.

Be certain you can restore items from the Recycle Bin.

IMPROVING YOUR WRITING SKILLS: GRAMMAR WORKSHOP

One of the most common errors made in business writing is noun and pronoun agreement. A noun must agree with the pronoun to which it refers both in person and number. If you are not sure if a pronoun is singular or plural, you should refer to a grammar reference manual.

For Review

Appendix: Rule 19: Noun and Pronoun Agreement

Directions

Write *C* at the end of the sentence if the use of nouns and pronouns is correct. Otherwise, make the necessary corrections.

Rule 19: Noun and Pronoun Agreement

1. Each of our field supervisors sends in their daily report for review.

2. The computer, as well as the software and CDs, has been ordered and they will be shipped next week.

3. These types of things happen, but we should prevent it from reoccurring.

4. Each computer must display their serial number.

5. Everything will be fine if it operates well.

6. Neither Celia nor Demetrius were planning to take their car to the party.

7. They were someone we could really depend on working hard for us.

8. Every one of the employees had their new office furniture.

9. The company announced their stock would split.

10. The employees were thrilled about their raise.

BANK RECONCILIATION FORM

1. **Compare your checking or savings register with your statement.** Put a check mark (√) in your register beside each check, deposit, or bank card transaction that appears on your statement. Be sure all amounts in your register match those on your statement. Assume for this problem this has been done and is correct.

2. **Identify outstanding checks or withdrawals.** List any checks or withdrawals you've written that have not yet appeared on your statement, and total the list in the column provided. (Hint: Use your tab key to move from column to column.)

Check Number	Dollars	
Total		

3. **Identify deposits made after your statement date.**

Deposit Date	Dollars	
Total		

4.	**Balance in checkbook**	
5.	**Subtract service charge**	
	Minus amount of service charge	
	Adjusted checkbook balance	
6.	**Balance in bank account**	
	a. Ending balance shown on bank statement	
	b. Plus deposits made after statement date (from step 3)	
	c. A plus B	
	d. Minus total of outstanding checks (from step 2)	
	e. C minus D (Total should match register balance)	

	f. If the adjusted bank statement balance and the adjusted checkbook balance do not agree, follow these steps.	
	1. Find the difference between the two.	
	2. Check the bank reconciliation to make certain you have made no errors.	
	3. Look for omissions of checks or deposits.	
	4. Check for a math error in the check stubs.	

PETTY CASH ENVELOPE

Petty Cash Fund		Date	No.	Explanation	Distribution of Payments		
Received	Paid Out				Supplies	Postage	Miscellaneous

NAME
DATE

Amount _____ No. _____

PETTY CASH VOUCHER

For _____

Paid to _____

Charge to _____

Date _____

Approved by _____

FORM 9-B-1

Amount _____ No. _____

PETTY CASH VOUCHER

For _____

Paid to _____

Charge to _____

Date _____

Approved by _____

FORM 9-B-2

Amount _____ No. _____

PETTY CASH VOUCHER

For _____

Paid to _____

Charge to _____

Date _____

Approved by _____

FORM 9-B-3

Amount _____ No. _____

PETTY CASH VOUCHER

For _____

Paid to _____

Charge to _____

Date _____

Approved by _____

FORM 9-B-4

Amount _____ No. _____

PETTY CASH VOUCHER

For _____

Paid to _____

Charge to _____

Date _____

Approved by _____

FORM 9-B-5

Amount _____ No. _____

PETTY CASH VOUCHER

For _____

Paid to _____

Charge to _____

Date _____

Approved by _____

FORM 9-B-6

7

Amount _____ No. _____

PETTY CASH VOUCHER

For _____

Paid to _____

Charge to _____

Date _____

Approved by _____

FORM 9-B-7

Amount _____ No. _____

PETTY CASH VOUCHER

For _____

Paid to _____

Charge to _____

Date _____

Approved by _____

FORM 9-B-8

Amount _____ No. _____

PETTY CASH VOUCHER

For _____

Paid to _____

Charge to _____

Date _____

Approved by _____

FORM 9-B-9

Amount _____ No. _____

PETTY CASH VOUCHER

For _____

Paid to _____

Charge to _____

Date _____

Approved by _____

FORM 9-B-10

Amount _____ No. _____

PETTY CASH VOUCHER

For _____

Paid to _____

Charge to _____

Date _____

Approved by _____

FORM 9-B-11

Amount _____ No. _____

PETTY CASH VOUCHER

For _____

Paid to _____

Charge to _____

Date _____

Approved by _____

FORM 9-B-12

WEEKLY PAYROLL REGISTER

For Week Ending: ___July July 22, 20xx___

Name	Marital Status	Withholding Allowance	Hourly Rate	Reg Hrs	Overtime Hrs	Regular Earnings	Overtime Earnings	Gross Earnings	OASDI	HI	Federal Income Tax	Group Med Ins	Group Dental Ins	Total Deductions	Net Pay
Brown, J. K.	M	3	13.00	40	8						38.00	22.00	13.00		
Caton, L. M.	M	1	10.80	40	5						31.00	38.00	8.00		
Rodriguez, J. L.	M	1	11.00	40	9						42.00	41.00	11.00		
Thai, J. T.	M	1	12.25	40	12						61.00	22.00	5.00		
Ussery, D. A.	M	3	14.00	40	3						30.00	12.00	8.00		
Venzor, L. T.	M	2	10.00	40	2						16.00	41.00	10.00		
Williams, O. M.	M	2	9.00	40	4						14.00	38.00	11.00		
Yancy, K. K.	M	0	13.00	40	5						55.00	22.00	8.00		
Yeamon, B. E.	M	0	11.00	40	9						51.00	38.00	13.00		
Yeoman, E. A.	M	4	12.50	40	12						36.00	38.00	10.00		
Totals															

IMPROVING YOUR WRITING SKILLS: GRAMMAR WORKSHOP

Keeping your grammar skills sharp requires constant attention to sentence analysis. Don't try to apply all rules at one time when proofreading for grammar errors. There are too many rules, and it is easy to overlook an error. Read each sentence carefully looking for mistakes using one specific rule. With practice, errors will quickly become apparent to you and proofreading will take less time.

For Review

Appendix: Rule 20: Parallel Construction

Directions

Write *C* at the end of the sentence if the grammar is correct. Otherwise, make the necessary corrections.

Rule 20: Parallel Construction

1. The customer service representative is determined to help the unhappy customer and is open to all suggestions.

2. The disgruntled employees filled the lunchroom and continued with their discussions.

3. She said that she had studied the report and refers it to the central office.

4. We have three stated goals: to increase production, to expand our market, and recruiting qualified workers.

5. He smelled the gaseous odor when he opened the door.

6. Luisita said the class was interesting, helpful, but it was too long.

7. Several students planned to meet in the student center, to review for the test, and as a result they worked hard.

8. Susan went to make copies of her report, a restaurant, and to get gas for her car.

9. I think both talking and to listen shows you are interested in the other person.

10. We are not for listening to office gossip nor complaining about the supervisor.

APPOINTMENT CALENDAR

Amanda Quevedo

DATE _____

TIME	APPOINTMENTS
8:00	
8:20	
8:40	
9:00	
9:20	
9:40	
10:00	
10:20	
10:40	
11:00	
11:20	
11:40	
12:00	
1:00	
1:20	
1:40	
2:00	
2:20	
2:40	
3:00	
3:20	
3:40	
4:00	
4:20	
4:40	

REMINDERS

NAME
DATE

FORM 10-A-1

APPOINTMENT CALENDAR

Student Name: _____

DATE _____

TIME	APPOINTMENTS
8:00	
8:20	
8:40	
9:00	
9:20	
9:40	
10:00	
10:20	
10:40	
11:00	
11:20	
11:40	
12:00	
1:00	
1:20	
1:40	
2:00	
2:20	
2:40	
3:00	
3:20	
3:40	
4:00	
4:20	
4:40	

REMINDERS

NAME
DATE

IMPROVING YOUR WRITING SKILLS: GRAMMAR WORKSHOP

Taking time to review grammar principles or rules will help you gain confidence in communicating clearly. The ability to use correct grammar is essential for an office assistant's success.

For Review

Appendix: Rule 21: Make Modifiers Clear

Directions

Write *C* at the end of the sentences if the grammar is correct. Otherwise, make the necessary corrections.

Rule 21: Make Modifiers Clear

1. Jason drew a design for his supervisor on the board.

2. Working hard last weekend, the computer program was completed.

3. Being busy, I helped Grady to finish the project.

4. Mary found Jane in the drawer with all of her files.

5. Since his logic is faulty, Ted helped Gordon find the solutions.

6. Notices on bulletin boards inform employees of their rights throughout the facility.

7. Slipping on the ice, his leg was injured.

8. Turning on the fan, his papers flew on the floor.

9. The missing purchase requisitions were found by her assistant lying on the floor.

10. Skilled with software applications, the human resources offered Maxine Rogers a position in the sales department.

NOTES ON MS. QUEVEDO'S TRIP TO SOUTHWESTERN REGION

Appointments

Tuesday, September 2

> 9 a.m.–11 a.m. Art Jacobs, manager of small appliance sales,
> Southwestern Region.

> 2 p.m. James Taylor, manager of refrigerator sales, Southwestern
> Region.

Wednesday, September 3

> Visit the manufacturing plant of Supreme Appliances, Inc., in Fort
> Worth. Contact is A. C. Matlock, vice president, manufacturing.

Thursday, September 4

> 10 a.m. L. C. Appleton, speaker at the November sales seminar.
> Meeting will take place at the University of Houston, Management
> Building, Room 326.

> 8 p.m. Speak to the Sales Management Club, University of Houston.

Lunch and dinner appointments

Monday, September 1

> 8 p.m. Take Mr. and Mrs. Reddin to dinner at Sweeney's Restaurant.

Tuesday, September 2

> 12:00 Lunch with Mr. Reddin and Mr. Jacobs.

NAME

DATE

7:30 p.m. Dinner at Sweeney's. Ms. Quevedo's guests: Mr. and Mrs. James Taylor, Mr. and Mrs. John Smith, and Mr. and Mrs. Art Jacobs.

Wednesday, September 3

Lunch with Mr. Matlock.

Thursday, September 4

Lunch with Mr. Appleton.

Hotel reservations

Americana Inn of the Six Flags for September 1 and 2; at the Americana Hotel in Houston for September 3 and 4. (Hotel confirmations are in envelope with airline tickets.)

Travel plans

Monday, September 1

2:15 p.m. Leave Rochester Airport on AA Flight 613 to Chicago. (One-hour wait in Chicago.) AA Flight 272 from Chicago to DFW. Mr. John Reddin, manager, Southwestern Region, will meet Ms. Quevedo at DFW.

Wednesday, September 3

Drive to Fort Worth. Car reserved with Hertz. Car is to be delivered to Inn of the Six Flags at 8 a.m. Wednesday.

At 3 p.m. drive to DFW. Take AA Flight 314 to Houston. (Prof. Agnes Wiggins, professor of Marketing, University of Houston, will meet Ms. Quevedo at the Houston Airport. Prof. Wiggins will also pick Ms. Quevedo up at 6:15 p.m. on Thursday at the Americana Hotel to drive to the University of Houston in time for the Sales Management Club banquet at 7:00 p.m.)

Friday, September 5

Take AA Flight 312 to Chicago at 9:15 a.m. (Take courtesy van from Americana Hotel to airport.)

Arrive in Chicago at 12:09 p.m.

1:17 p.m. Leave Chicago on AA Flight 416 for Rochester.

Additional Information

Thursday afternoon

Ms. Quevedo goes back to the Americana to put finishing touches on her speech for the Sales Management Club.

Expense Reimbursement Voucher

DRAFT

Name: _Sheryl Robinson_   Department: _Sales_

For Period Beginning _5-4---_   Ending _5-9---_

Purpose of Business Trip: Sales Exposition - Southwest Region

			5-4	5-5	5-6	5-7	5-8	5-9	Total
Destination	From		Dallas		New Orl	Dallas	Dallas		
	To		New Orl		Dallas	Ft Worth	Dallas		
Transportation	Car Travel	Mileage				58 mi	35 mi		120
		Rate × Miles				23 38	9 63		33 01
		Car Rentals	24 00		37 48				61 48
		Parking	7 00	7 00	7 00	4 00			25 00
		Tolls				1 00	1 00		2 00
	Air Fare (RT)		243 76						243 76
	Rail Fare								
	Carfare & Bus								
	Limousine/Taxi		10 00		10 00				20 00
	Tips		2 00		2 00				4 00
Hotel	Room Charge		78 97	78 97					157 94
	Hotel Tips		2 00		2 00				4 00
Misc.	Postage						1 95		1 95
	Telephone/Telegrams		1 50	4 95	3 80	50	75		11 50
	Laundry				9 40				9 40
	Other, Attach Statement								
	Subtotal								
Meals and Entertainment	Meals on travel status		15 75	36 80					52 55
	Meals w/bus. discussion*				39 00	14 00			53 00
	Other bus. entertainment*		8 00	14 00			5 50		27 50
	Subtotal								
	Meals w/ no bus. discussion								
	Total		392 98	141 72	110 68	42 88	18 83		707 09

		Less Amount Advanced	500 00
		Balance Due	214 84

I certify these travel expenses were incurred by me in the transaction of authorized company business

Signature _Sheryl Robinson_

* (explain on reverse side)

FORM 11-D

Expense Reimbursement Voucher

FINAL

Name ___Sheryl Robinson___

For Period Beginning ___5-4- - -___ Ending ___5-9- - -___

Department ___Sales___

Purpose of Business Trip: Sales Exposition - Southwest Region

Date		5-4	5-5	5-6	5-7	5-8	5-9	Total	C/I
Destination From		Dallas		New Orl	Dallas	Dallas			
To		New Orl	Dallas	Dallas	Ft Worth	Dallas			
Transportation — Car Travel — Mileage					58 mi	35 mi		120	1.
Rate × Miles					23 38	9 63		33 01	2.
Car Rentals		24 00		37 48				61 48	3.
Parking		7 00	7 00	7 00	4 00			25 00	4.
Tolls					1 00	1 00		2 00	5.
Air Fare (RT)		243 76						243 76	6.
Rail Fare									
Carfare & Bus									
Limousine/Taxi		10 00		10 00				20 00	7.
Tips		2 00		2 00				4 00	8.
Hotel — Room Charge		78 97	78 97					157 94	9.
Hotel Tips		2 00		2 00				4 00	10.
Misc. — Postage						1 95		1 95	11.
Telephone/Telegrams		1 50	4 95	3 80	50	75		11 50	12.
Laundry				9 40				9 40	13.
Other, Attach Statement									
Subtotal									
Meals and Entertainment — Meals on travel status		15 75	36 80					52 55	14.
Meals w/bus. discussion*				39 00	14 00			53 00	15.
Other bus. entertainment*		8 00	14 00			5 50		27 50	16.
Subtotal									
Meals w/ no bus. discussion									
Total		392 98	141 72	110 68	42 88	18 83		707 09	17.

I certify these travel expenses were incurred by me in the transaction of authorized company business

Less Amount Advanced ___500 00___

Signature _____

Balance Due ___214 84___   18.

*(explain on reverse side)

FORM 11-D-1

IMPROVING YOUR WRITING SKILLS: GRAMMAR WORKSHOP

Taking time to review grammar principles or rules will help you gain confidence in communicating clearly. The ability to use correct grammar is essential for an office assistant's success.

For Review

Appendix: Rule 22: Use Adjectives and Adverbs Correctly

Directions

Select the correct word in parentheses by underlining it.

Rule 22: Use Adjectives and Adverbs Correctly

1. She played the piano (beautiful, beautifully).

2. They did such a terrific job on the proposal that they were commended for doing (good, well).

3. They were told to move very (quick, quickly) when the portable walls were moved.

4. His supervisor felt (bad, badly) that there were no merit increases.

5. You will need a (considerable, considerably) larger supply of ribbons and diskettes.

6. Please don't take what I say (personal, personally.)

7. The apple tastes (sweet, sweetly).

8. The office runs much (smoother, smoothly) that it did when we had less space.

9. Sophia looks (good, well) since she has returned from her leave of absence.

10. The policeman's uniform looks (good, well) on him.

November Sales Meeting Notes

Meeting of Executive Committee for November Sales Seminar
Wednesday, Sept. 10, 5 p.m.
Ms. Quevedo's office
All members present.

Announcement: Sid Levine has agreed to help with the Nov. Sales Seminar. He will be responsible for registration.

The minutes of the August meeting of the Executive Committee were distributed. One correction was called for. Honorariums will be paid to the keynote speaker and the banquet speaker but not to the luncheon speakers. The minutes were approved as corrected.

James Bradford proposed that the keynote speaker and the banquet speaker each be paid an honorarium of $500. Committee members agreed.

Lisa Rogers reported that James Atwell, who is in charge of working with the hotel on setting up audiovisual equipment, is ill and has asked to be relieved of this responsibility. Whom shall we ask to do this? After some discussion, Mr. Bradford volunteered for the job.

Louise Witherspoon reported that increased attendance at the seminar (over attendance of previous years) is anticipated. Therefore, some of the meeting rooms that have been assigned to the sectional meetings of the Nov. Sales Seminar may be too small. She raised the question: Should we ask for larger rooms? The Executive Committee instructed her to check with the hotel to see if larger rooms are available and, if so, to make arrangements to shift the large sectional meetings to larger rooms. Be sure to give the information on room changes to A. C. Rothbaum, who is responsible for having the program printed. He needs the room changes by Sept. 20.

Meeting adjourned, 6:30 p.m.

A. Quevedo

MEETING CHECKLIST

BEFORE THE MEETING		
General	**Target Date**	**Completion Date**
Secure names/addresses		
Reserve meeting room(s)		
Make calendar notations		
Prepare meeting notice		
Prepare agenda		
Send notice/agenda		
Prepare list of materials, supplies, equipment needed		
Order refreshments (or meal)		
Prepare meeting evaluation forms		
Prepare handouts		
Make hotel reservation(s)		
Confirm meeting room(s)		
Meeting Room(s)		
Location of electrical outlets		
Extension cords		
Audiovisual equipment		
Audiovisual supplies		
Name tags/name cards		
Seating arrangements		
Arrange for water pitcher/glasses		
Arrange for pads/pens		
THE MEETING DAY		
Final check on meeting room(s)		
Final check on food		
Final check on equipment		
AFTER THE MEETING		
Prepare/distribute notes/minutes		
Prepare follow-up correspondence		
Summarize evaluation forms		

IMPROVING YOUR WRITING SKILLS: GRAMMAR WORKSHOP

A common error in business writing is the overuse of passive voice sentences. You should write using the active voice by having the subject of the sentence completing the action.

For Review

Appendix: Rule 23: Choose Active Voice over Passive Voice in Business Writing

Directions

Rewrite each passive sentence to make it an active sentence. Write a **C** at the end of the sentence if the sentence is already active.

Rule 23: Active and Passive Voice

1. PowerPoint and Access were installed on Jeffrey's computer by Hillary on Monday.

2. The manager's and her assistant's calendars are updated by the assistant before she leaves each day.

3. Office supplies were ordered by the accounting department for July.

4. The media director was informed by Ruben the meeting had been cancelled.

5. Twice this week John repaired the air-conditioning after it went out in our building.

6. Printers that will print, scan, and fax were ordered by the business department.

7. Tai and Joshua completed the team project before the deadline.

8. The information report on making presentations was researched and composed on time for the June issue of the newsletter.

9. Rarely do we have to edit the work done by Rita.

10. Our department will reach its goal for United Way if we collect $300.

SPEECH ANXIETY SELF-ASSESSMENT

Directions: Place a check mark in the blank that best describes how you feel.

When I stand before an audience, I:	Never	Sometimes	Quite Often	Always
Begin perspiring.				
Feel relaxed and at ease.				
Wish I were anywhere but here.				
Imagine myself giving a good speech.				
Feel weak in the knees.				
Know that only I know I am afraid.				
Accept that no one is perfect at this.				
Feel as if I will faint.				
Hear my heart pounding.				
Can psych myself to a positive mood.				
Feel my knees shaking.				
Don't mind giving presentations.				
Have a dry, constricted throat.				
Will only think positive thoughts.				
Hear my voice quivering.				
Know you are what you think.				
Know my face is flushed.				
Believe I can get through this.				
Am going to forget half of my speech.				
Know I will end up doing well.				

IMPROVING YOUR WRITING SKILLS: GRAMMAR WORKSHOP

Taking time to review grammar principles or rules will help you gain confidence in communicating clearly. The ability to use correct grammar is essential for an office professional's success.

For Review

Appendix: Rule 24: Plurals and Possessives

Directions

Write *C* at the end of the sentences if the grammar is correct. Otherwise, make the necessary corrections.

1. At first, both boards of directors were unwilling to accept the recommendations for management changes.

2. In the past month, at least three employees in the Sales Division took leaves of absence.

3. What percentage of the CEO's were women over 45 years old?.

4. At least 20 percent of their community college graduates earn A.A.S.s in business administration.

5. All CPAs must earn non-credits every three years.

6. Juan was told he could earn 3.8 percent on six month's interest.

7. Because of a data entry difficulty, all of the customers' addresses were reentered into the database.

8. In just one days' voice mail system, Janie receives as many as ten messages.

9. Success depends on an organization's commitment to its employees.

10. The employee's difficulties lie in their lack of supporting their company's mission.

VALUE CLARIFICATION

Value	Identify your value with a check mark	Prioritize with 1–5, with 1 being the top priority
Hard-working, aspiring		
Open-minded to new ideas, changes		
Lighthearted, sense of humor		
Neat, tidy, well organized		
Speaks up to support beliefs		
Willing to forgive others		
Works for the benefit of the team		
Sincere, truthful		
Imaginative, creative		
Independent, self-reliant		
Intellectual, reflective		
Logical, consistent		
Respectful		
Polite, courteous		
Dependable, reliable		
Self-disciplined		

NAME
DATE

FORM 14-A